WEATHER
AND
CLIMATE!

Kathleen M. Reilly

Illustrated by Tom Casteel

Titles in the **Explore Earth Science** Set

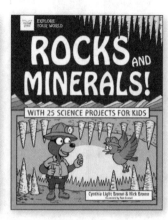

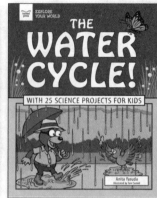

Check out more titles at www.nomadpress.net

Nomad Press

A division of Nomad Communications

10 9 8 7 6 5 4 3 2 1

This book was manufactured by Versa Press, East Peoria, Illinois
February 2020, Job #J19-11230
ISBN Softcover: 978-1-61930-866-4
ISBN Hardcover: 978-1-61930-863-3

Educational Consultant, Marla Conn

Questions regarding the ordering of this book should be addressed to
Nomad Press
2456 Christian St., White River Junction, VT 05001
www.nomadpress.net

Printed in the United States.

CONTENTS

Interested in primary sources? Look for this icon. Use a smartphone or tablet app to scan the QR code and explore more! Photos are also primary sources because a photograph takes a picture at the moment something happens.

You can find a list of URLs on the Resources page. If the QR code doesn't work, try searching the internet with the Keyword Prompts to find other helpful sources.

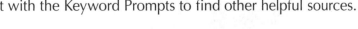

→ 🔎 EXPLORE WEATHER AND CLIMATE

RAIN

If a raindrop falls the average speed of 14 miles per hour from a cloud of average height of 2,500 feet, it would take the drop two minutes to hit the ground!

DROUGHT

As the climate warms, scientists expect droughts to happen more often and last longer.

GLACIER

The largest glacier on Earth is the Lambert glacier in Antarctica, which is 60 miles wide and about 270 miles long!

RAINFOREST

Rainforests cover about 2 percent of the earth's surface, but about 50 percent of all plants and animals on Earth live in a rainforest.

DESERT

Areas covered in ice or snow are called "cold deserts," compared to hot deserts in warm areas. Antarctica is the largest cold desert on Earth.

HURRICANE

Hurricanes have different names—in the Atlantic Ocean they are hurricanes, in the Northwest Pacific Ocean they are typhoons, and in the South Pacific and Indian Oceans they are cyclones.

INTRODUCTION

WHAT IS WEATHER AND CLIMATE?

Imagine it's Saturday morning. You wake up and get dressed to go outside. You pull on some shorts and a T-shirt and run out the door into—snow. Oops! You didn't think about what the weather was going to be like.

Of course, it's unusual for there to be snow when you think it's going to be warm. But weather is a major part of our daily lives, affecting what we wear and do. You might picture summer as always sunny and hot. But it can rain during the summer or even be chilly. Severe weather—such as a thunderstorm—can rattle a calm summer afternoon. In hazardous weather, such as a tornado, you need to get to a safe place.

1

WORDS TO KNOW

climate: the average weather in an area during a long period of time.

equator: the imaginary line around the earth halfway between the North and South Poles.

region: a large area of the earth.

weather pattern: repeating weather during a number of days or weeks or months.

desert: an area that lacks water, receiving 10 inches or less of precipitation each year.

The weather you experience depends on where you live, and it can vary quite a lot from day to day. The climate is the average type of weather a place gets during the entire year and longer.

WHAT IS CLIMATE?

You may live in an area that gets a ton of snow in the winter. But your cousin might live nearer to the equator, where it's hot and they wear shorts for most of the year.

What's up? Why the difference? Different regions have different weather patterns. What we call "weather" is really something that we measure during a short period of time—was it raining yesterday or last week? Is it hot today? Climate is measured during the course of many, many years.

When you think of Africa, what kind of weather do you think of? Probably hot and dry. What about the North Pole? Brr! Cold and snowy. That's the climate of those areas. But on any one day, it could rain in the desert of Africa or even be chilly. That's called weather. But the general trend, or climate, is hot and dry.

WHAT KIND OF METEOR CAN PREDICT THE WEATHER? *A meteorologist.*

PREDICTING THE WEATHER

Have you ever turned on the computer, television, or radio and heard someone telling you what the weather will be for the week? People who study the weather are called meteorologists.

Meteorologists observe what is happening in the atmosphere, including the movement of air masses, changing temperatures, and rising and falling air pressure. They use these observations to predict what the weather will be like in an hour, tomorrow, or next week.

Accurate weather predictions are important for planning. Farmers need to know when to plant their crops. Airlines need to know if it will be safe to fly. Schools need to know if classes should be canceled.

But there are so many things that go into figuring out what the weather is going to do that even meteorologists can get it wrong. Sometimes, meteorologists forecast that it's going to rain buckets, and you end up with a day of only drizzle! It's not an exact science.

meteorologist: a person who studies the science of weather and climate.

atmosphere: the blanket of air surrounding the earth.

air mass: a large pocket of air that is different from the air around it.

air pressure: the force of the gases surrounding the earth pressing downward.

predict: to say what will happen in the future.

crop: a plant grown for food and other uses.

forecast: to make a prediction of the weather.

WORDS ⊙ KNOW

Learn more about the difference between weather and climate in this video.

🔍 CRASH COURSE WEATHER →

WORDS TO KNOW

altitude: the height above the level of the sea. Also called elevation.

humidity: the amount of moisture in the air.

LOOKS LIKE NICE WEATHER!

Before there were any weather instruments, people simply observed nature to predict the weather. Some of these observations turned out to be quite accurate! People even thought up sayings to help them remember the predictions. Take a look!

"Dew on the grass, no rain will pass." If it didn't rain overnight, check the grass in the morning. If it's dry, that means strong breezes have already dried the dew. Strong breezes often mean rain. If the grass is still wet with dew, there's no wind and it probably won't rain.

"Halo around the moon or sun, rain is coming on the run." A ring around the sun or moon is created by light passing through ice crystals at high **altitude**. When moisture is that high in the atmosphere, it means an active weather system bringing rain or snow is heading your way quickly.

"When leaves show their undersides, be very sure that rain betides." **Humidity** can soften some leaves, making them curl or turn over. Humidity indicates that rain could be on the way. But this saying only works for certain kinds of trees, such as oak and poplar.

"When the wind is from the east, 'tis neither good for man nor beast." The wind is a great indicator of weather. To find out which way the wind is blowing, toss a piece of grass in the air. If the wind is from the east, it means rain is coming. If it's very strong from the east, a storm is coming.

"Crickets can tell the temperature." If you hear a cricket chirping, count how many times it chirps in 14 seconds. Add 40 to that number. The total should be close to the actual temperature, in Fahrenheit. (For Celsius, count 25 seconds, then divide by three, and add four.)

barometer: a weather instrument that measures air pressure.

anemometer: a weather instrument that measures wind speed.

WORDS ⊚ KNOW

⋯ DID YOU KNOW? ⋯⋯⋯

Before computers, weather forecasters predicted the weather using mechanical instruments such as barometers **and** anemometers **and by looking outside.**

In this book, you'll explore all these things—and more. You'll learn why some areas have different weather patterns than others, and how weather forecasts can predict the weather.

You'll discover what makes snow, rain, and sleet, and what clouds and rainbows are all about. And you'll learn how to build your own weather instruments, teach your family and friends how to stay safe from extreme weather, and even eat some clouds!

So, turn the page and let's start exploring the amazing world of weather and climate!

THIS SCIENTIST IS WATCHING FOR HURRICANES!
U.S. AIR FORCE PHOTO BY MAJ. MARNEE A.C. LOSURDO

GOOD SCIENCE PRACTICES

Every good scientist keeps a science journal! Choose a notebook to use as your science journal. Write down your ideas, observations, and comparisons as you read this book.

For each project in this book, make and use a scientific method worksheet, like the one shown here. Scientists use the scientific method to keep their experiments organized. A scientific method worksheet will help you keep track of your observations and results.

Each chapter of this book begins with a question to help guide your exploration of weather and climate.

Scientific Method Worksheet

Question: What are we trying to find out? What problem are we trying to solve?

Research: What information is already known?

Hypothesis/Prediction: What do I think the answer will be?

Equipment: What supplies do I need?

Method: What steps will I follow?

Results: What happened? Why?

? INVESTIGATE!

What is the climate like where you live?

Keep the question in your mind as you read the chapter. Record your thoughts, questions, and observations in your science journal. At the end of each chapter, use your science journal to record your thoughts and answers. Does your answer change as you read the chapter?

PROJECT!

EDIBLE CLIMATE ZONE MAP

SUPPLIES

* pizza dough and pizza toppings such as sauce, olives, pepperoni, pineapple, different cheeses, bell peppers
* rolling pin
* baking sheets

The world has many different types of climates. The United States has several different climate zones **as well. With this edible map, you can tell your family about summer climates—after you chew!**

Caution: Have an adult help you with the oven!

1 Take a good look at this climate zone map of the United States shown here. Roll out your dough and cut it into the shape of the United States. It doesn't have to be perfect!

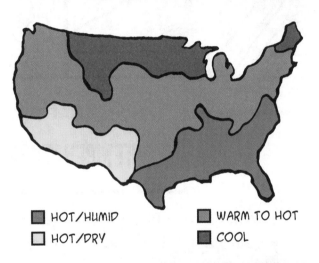

■ HOT/HUMID   ■ WARM TO HOT
□ HOT/DRY   ■ COOL

2 Cover the entire country with sauce and a layer of cheese.

3 Now you're ready to create your summer climates. There are four general climate areas in the United States: hot/humid, hot/dry, warm to hot, and cool. Use one topping for each climate area.

THINK ABOUT IT: If you moved to a different climate zone, what might you have to change about your life in the new climate? Would your daily activities be different? Your clothing? What about the car your family drives?

4 Bake the pizza until the cheese is starting to brown. Share your climate zone meal with your family!

WORDS TO KNOW

climate zone: a large region with a similar climate.

7

CHAPTER 1

TEMPERATURE TIPS

What's your favorite time of year? Maybe you like the
summer, when you can spend long days outside, go
swimming, and eat ice-cold popsicles. Maybe it's autumn,
when you can pick apples and crunch through fallen leaves.
Do you like to zoom down hills on skis in winter or plant
a garden in the spring? As the temperature changes along
with the seasons, so do your favorite outdoor activities.

A big part of the weather you experience every day is the
temperature. Is it too cold for short sleeves? Is it too warm for
a jacket? When studying the
weather, temperature is a key
thing to know!

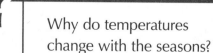

? **INVESTIGATE!**

Why do temperatures
change with the seasons?

WHAT'S THE TEMPERATURE?

How do you know what the temperature is outside? You can look at a thermometer. Many thermometers today are digital, but older thermometers are made from glass tubes that contain mercury. When it's hot, the mercury warms up and expands, rising up the tube. When it's cold, the mercury contracts and drops down the tube.

Temperature is measured on three different scales.

✳ **FAHRENHEIT:** In the United States, people use Fahrenheit to measure temperature. On this scale, water freezes at 32 degrees and boils at 212 degrees.

✳ **CELSIUS:** In most countries, people use Celsius to measure temperature. On the Celsius scale, water freezes at 0 degrees and boils at 100 degrees.

✳ **KELVIN:** Scientists use a scale called Kelvin. On this scale, 0 is the coldest possible temperature anything can be. Water freezes at 273 degrees and boils at 373 degrees.

A TRADITIONAL THERMOMETER

WORDS ⊙ KNOW

temperature: a measure of warmth or coldness, using a standard value scale.

thermometer: a weather instrument used to measure temperature.

digital: an electronic way of presenting information as numbers.

mercury: a liquid metal used inside thermometers.

expand: to spread out and take up more space.

contract: to shrink and take up less space.

scale: a measuring system.

⋯ **DID YOU KNOW?** ⋯

The highest temperature ever recorded was 136 degrees Fahrenheit (58 degrees Celsius) in Libya, a country in northern Africa. That's a scorcher!

WEATHER AND CLIMATE!

evaporate: to convert from a liquid to a gas.

heat index: the air temperature combined with the humidity in the air.

heat stroke: a condition when your body gets dangerously overheated.

species: a group of plants or animals that are closely related and produce offspring.

adapt: to make a change to better survive in the environment.

environment: a natural area with animals, plants, rocks, soil, and water.

WORDS ⏤ KNOW

I'M SO HOT!

Sometimes, the temperature on the thermometer might not seem that high, but you feel very hot. If the air contains a lot of moisture, it's humid. Humidity can make you feel as though it's even hotter than the temperature of the air.

When you're hot, you sweat. It's your body's way of getting rid of extra heat. Usually, the sweat on your skin evaporates into the air around you. If it's very humid, the moisture on your skin won't evaporate as well, making it harder to cool down.

To understand what the air outside will really feel like, scientists developed the heat index. The heat index combines the air temperature and the humidity. A very high heat index can lead to heat stroke. Your heart starts to pound fast and you feel dizzy. You need to get help if you feel the symptoms of heat stroke on a very hot day.

HOME SWEET HOME

Plants and animals live in every type of climate, from lush rainforests to hot, dry deserts to icy-cold polar regions. But you won't find a camel in the rainforest or a cactus in the Arctic. That's because plant and animal **species** have **adapted** to live in specific **environments**. They can't survive extreme changes. What about humans? How have humans adapted to survive in every climate?

advisory: an official announcement or warning.

wind chill: what the combination of air temperature and wind feels like on your skin.

WORDS TO KNOW

Fortunately, weather forecasters issue warnings to let you know when it's going to be a dangerously hot day.

✳ **A HEAT** advisory means that, within the next 12 to 24 hours, the heat index is expected to be greater than 105 degrees Fahrenheit (40 degrees Celsius) and less than 109 degrees Fahrenheit (42 degrees Celsius).

✳ **AN EXCESSIVE HEAT WARNING** means that, within the next 12 to 24 hours, the heat index may reach 110 degrees Fahrenheit (43 degrees Celsius) or greater.

✳ **AN EXCESSIVE HEAT WATCH** means that, within the next 24 to 48 hours, the heat index may reach 110 degrees Fahrenheit (43 degrees Celsius) or greater.

··· DID YOU KNOW? ·········

Temperature is affected by the ocean and by altitude. Juneau, Alaska, has more warm days than Flagstaff, Arizona. That's because Juneau is warmed by its location near the sea, while Flagstaff is cooled by its higher elevation.

IT'S SO COLD OUT!

If you live where winters are cold, you won't be worrying about the heat index. Instead, you will be bundling up to stay warm! And winter has its own measurement of how it really feels when you're outside—the wind chill.

You've probably noticed that you feel cooler when it's windy. The wind chill combines the temperature of the air with the amount of wind. Suppose it's 5 degrees Fahrenheit (-15 degrees Celsius) outside. That's pretty cold! But if the wind is blowing at 5 miles per hour, then it feels like it's -4 degrees Fahrenheit (-20 Celsius). If the wind is blowing at 20 miles per hour, then it feels like -15 degrees Fahrenheit (-26 degrees Celsius)! See what a difference the wind can make?

Once again, weather forecasters have your back. They'll issue alerts to let you know when it's dangerously cold outside.

* **A WIND CHILL ADVISORY** means that the wind chill is expected to be -15 to -24 degrees Fahrenheit (-26 to -31 degrees Celsius).

* **A WIND CHILL WARNING** means that the wind chill is expected to be below -25 degrees Fahrenheit (below -32 degrees Celsius).

PUFF, PUFF, PUFF

Ever wonder why you can see your breath when it's cold outside? That's because your breath is warm and humid—it contains evaporated water. When your warm breath hits the cold air, the moisture in it instantly gets colder and **denser** and turns into **water vapor**. The result is the little cloud you see.

WHEN IT GETS COLD, YOU CAN SEE YOUR BREATH IN THE AIR!

CHANGING SEASONS

Why do we have spring, summer, autumn, and winter? Because the earth is tilted slightly as it follows its orbit around the sun. When one half of the earth is tipped facing the sun, the other half is tipped away from it.

In May, June, and July, it's summer in the Northern Hemisphere because the Northern Hemisphere is facing the sun more directly. Days are long and warm. Meanwhile, it's winter in the Southern Hemisphere, and the days are colder and there are fewer hours of daylight. In November, December, and January, the Southern Hemisphere is facing the sun more directly and has summer, while the Northern Hemisphere has winter.

WORDS ⊙ KNOW

orbit: the path a planet takes around the sun.

Northern Hemisphere: the half of the earth north of the equator.

Southern Hemisphere: the half of the earth south of the equator.

mild: not too hot and not too cold.

monsoon: a wind that brings heavy rainfall to southern Asia in summer.

(PS) **Listen to Bill Nye explain why we have seasons.**

🔎 BILL NYE SEASONS VIDEO

··· DID YOU KNOW? ····

In India, people recognize six seasons instead of four: spring, summer, monsoon, autumn, pre-winter, and winter. Each season is about two months long.

In spring and autumn, temperatures are mild in most places. Except for the equator, the rest of the earth is not facing the sun directly, so it's not as cold as winter or as hot as summer.

WEATHER AND CLIMATE!

CLIMATE ZONES

As we've seen, temperature varies from one region to another. In fact, there are several different climate zones around the world. Generally, they're separated by air temperatures and the amount of precipitation an area gets. The earth is divided into three basic climate zones: tropical, temperate, and polar.

TROPICAL: This zone lies along the earth's equator. The tropical zone is hotter than areas farther north and south of the equator because it gets the most direct sunlight. The climate in tropical zones can either be dry or humid—for example, a desert is very dry and a rainforest is very humid.

CAN YOU SPOT THE TROPICAL, TEMPERATE, AND POLAR REGIONS ON THIS IMAGE OF THE EARTH?

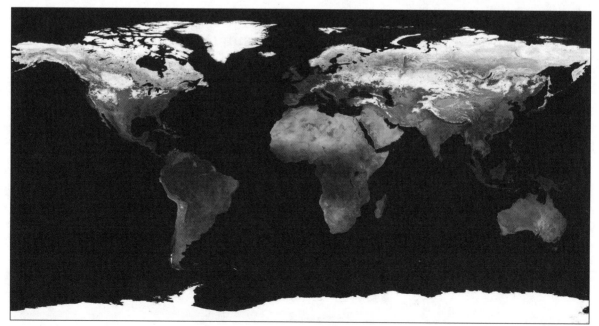

EXTREME CLIMATES

Some climates are extremely hot or cold. Desert regions, for example, experience very high temperatures. At night, though, the temperatures in some deserts can drop below freezing! That's because deserts have no trees, grass, or other plants to capture and hold the sun's heat from the day. Other extreme climates are found near the equator. They get more direct sunlight than anywhere else on Earth because the equator never tilts away from the sun. For example, because of its position along the equator, northern Africa gets almost constant sun and heat, with extremely little rainfall. On the other hand, polar regions get very little direct sunlight—if any. So the temperature can stay freezing for months.

WHAT KIND OF SHORTS DO CLOUDS WEAR?

Thunderwear!

TEMPERATE: Temperate zones have temperatures that may vary, but they don't get too hot or too cold for long. Most of the United States and Europe has a temperate climate.

POLAR: Polar zones can be found near the top and bottom of the earth. Antarctica, Alaska, and Greenland are all in a polar zone. These areas get the least direct sunlight, so their climates are the coldest.

Now that you know about temperature, let's take a look at another important part of weather—precipitation!

? CONSIDER AND DISCUSS

It's time to consider and discuss: Why do temperatures change with the seasons?

PROJECT!

MAKE A SUN CATCHER

Celebrate the sunshine coming in through the windows with a sun catcher! The sun is what creates a lot of the weather you experience.

1 Cover your work surface with a large piece of wax paper. Pour a little bit of glue onto a paper plate.

2 Cut a piece of yarn about a foot long and run it through the glue. Gently "pinch" off any excess glue by running the yarn between your finger and thumb. The yarn should have enough glue on it to make it stiff, but not dripping and sloppy.

3 Arrange your yarn on the wax paper in whatever shape you want, such as a star or a heart. Make

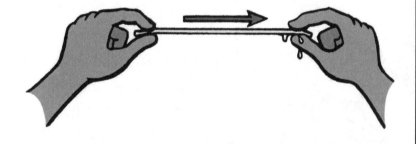

sure the ends of the yarn are touching each other so the shape is fully closed. Let it dry completely.

4 Cut a smaller piece of yarn. Once the shape is dry, carefully lift one edge of the shape and tie a short loop of yarn around it. This loop will be for hanging your sun catcher. Then, press your shape back down onto the wax paper. If it's lifting up even a little, glue will leak out during the next step.

5 Pour more glue on the paper plate and add a few drops of food coloring. Use the toothpick to blend the glue and food coloring. Then, pour the glue onto the wax paper inside your shape. Use the toothpick to push the glue around until the inside of your shape is completely filled.

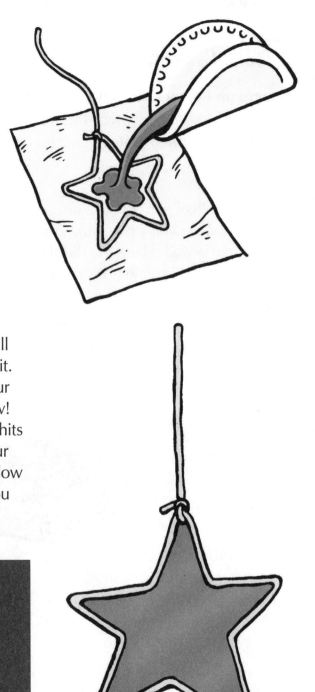

6 Let your sun catcher dry completely and then gently pull the wax paper off the back of it. Now, you're ready to hang your sun catcher in a sunny window! What happens when the light hits your design? Does moving your sun catcher to a different window change what you see when you hang it? Why?

TRY THIS! Make more shapes and divide them with yarn into more than one section. Make each section a different color.

PROJECT!

ANGLE OF THE SUN

SUPPLIES

* white paper
* freezer
* short stack of books, about 2 inches tall
* strong flashlight that produces some heat when it's shining
* clipboard
* science journal
* pencil

Places on the equator, where the sun shines directly, are very hot. Places where the sun shines at an angle, such as the United States, have less extreme heat. Let's see why.

1 Put the white paper in the freezer for about 15 minutes. Meanwhile, place the stack of books 2 inches away from a wall. Place the flashlight on the books and turn it on so it is shining directly at the wall.

2 Take the paper out of the freezer and quickly clip it to the clipboard. Prop up the clipboard against the wall so the flashlight is shining on it. Make it as straight as possible.

3 Draw a circle around the beam of light on the paper, trying not to touch any other part of the paper.

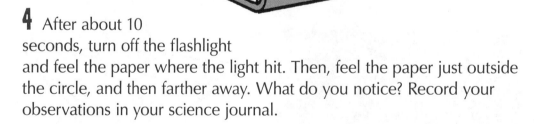
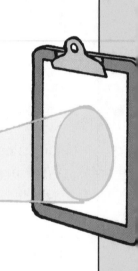

4 After about 10 seconds, turn off the flashlight and feel the paper where the light hit. Then, feel the paper just outside the circle, and then farther away. What do you notice? Record your observations in your science journal.

5 Put the paper back in the freezer. After 15 minutes, take it out and put it on the clipboard again.

PROJECT!

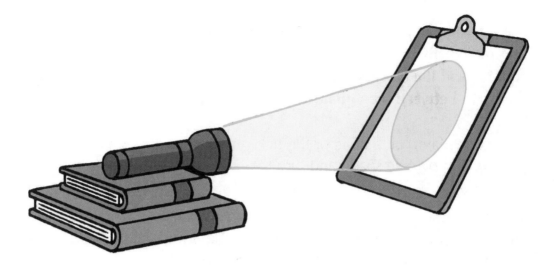

6 Prop the clipboard against the wall at an angle, so it tips away from the flashlight. Then, shine the flashlight on the paper and draw a circle around the beam of light again. Is the circle the same size as before?

7 After 10 seconds, turn off the light and feel the paper again. What do you notice this time?

THINK ABOUT IT: What does this show you about the tilt of the earth? Can you think of any place on the planet that might get no sun at all because of the sun's angle? What will the temperature be like there? What climate zone would that region be? What might people have to do to live there?

PROJECT!

MODEL THE SEASONS

See for yourself how the earth's tilt causes the seasons. Keep in mind that the Northern Hemisphere is the half of the earth between the equator and the North Pole and the Southern Hemisphere is the half the earth between the equator and the South Pole.

1 Place the lamp on a table or the floor, making sure it's on a stable surface. Remove the shade and turn the light on. This is your sun.

2 Facing the lamp, stand a couple of feet away holding the globe. This is your earth. Note where the North Pole is and where the South Pole is. Tip the globe slightly in your hands, so the North Pole is tilting toward the lamp. Look at how the light hits the globe. Which hemisphere is experiencing summer? Which is in winter?

3 Keeping the tilt at the same angle and facing in the same direction, move your earth **counterclockwise** one-quarter of the way around the sun. Which hemisphere is in spring and which is in autumn?

4 Keeping the tilt at the same angle and facing in the same direction, move your earth counterclockwise another quarter of the way around the light, so it is on the opposite side from where you started. The southern part of your globe is now tilted toward the sun and experiencing summer, and the northern part is tilted away, in winter.

5 Keeping the tilt at the same angle and facing in the same direction, finish the experiment by moving the globe another quarter of the way around the light. Where is it spring and where is it autumn now?

THINK ABOUT IT: How would your life be different if you had only one season where you live?

WORDS to KNOW

counterclockwise: in the opposite direction to the way the hands of a clock move.

20

PROJECT!

MAKE A THERMOMETER

Traditional thermometers work when the air temperature warms or cools the liquid inside the tube. When the liquid heats up, it expands and rises up the tube. When the liquid cools, it contracts and falls down the tube. See how this works.

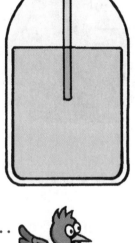

1 Fill the bottle about one-quarter full with a mix of half water and half rubbing alcohol. To make the liquid easier to see, add a few drops of food coloring.

2 Wrap a wad of clay around one end of the straw. Put the other end of the straw into the bottle, but don't let it touch the bottom. Slide the clay farther down the straw if you need to in order to keep it from touching the bottom.

3 Warm the liquid by holding the bottle very still between both of your hands. As the liquid gets warm, it expands. What happens to the liquid in the straw? Record your observations and make a sketch in your science journal.

⋯ DID YOU KNOW? ⋯

The lowest temperature ever recorded on Earth was -129 degrees Fahrenheit (-89.5 degrees Celsius) in Antarctica. Brrrr!

THINK ABOUT IT: If you didn't have a thermometer to tell you the temperature, what could you observe in nature that might give you an idea of what the temperature is?

CHAPTER 2

ALL ABOUT AIR PRESSURE

If you've ever watched a weather forecast on television, you've probably seen a big map with lots of lines and symbols. And maybe the meteorologist said something like, "An area of high pressure will be building up and moving over our area" or, "Expect an area of low pressure to overtake the region tomorrow."

Why should you care about the pressure? You just want to know whether to bring your rain jacket to school! But air pressure actually can tell us what kind of weather to expect.

? INVESTIGATE!

How does air pressure affect the weather?

When forecasters talk about air pressure, they're referring to how strongly the atmosphere is pressing down toward the surface of the earth. It's hard to believe air has any weight to press down on anything. After all, air is around you all the time, but you don't feel it.

Like mercury in a thermometer, warm air rises and cool air falls. The molecules in warm air start moving faster and spread farther apart. This makes the air less dense and lighter, so it rises.

Some places on Earth are always warmer than others. Air temperature is affected by time of day or night, the tilt of the earth, and the way different surfaces—such as rocks, trees, or water—absorb sunlight. Air is always moving around between areas of cold air and areas of warm air to try to even out its temperature. This movement causes changes in air pressure. And air pressure affects the weather.

WHAT'S THE OPPOSITE OF A COLD FRONT?

A warm back!

high pressure: an area in the atmosphere where the air pressure and density are above average.

low pressure: an area in the atmosphere where the air pressure is less dense than the surrounding air.

molecule: two or more atoms bound together. Atoms are very small pieces of matter that make up everything in the universe.

absorb: to soak up a liquid or take in energy, heat, light, or sound.

WORDS TO KNOW

BALLOONING

You can do a quick experiment with balloons to see that air has weight. If you hang two full balloons from each end of a stick and then hang the stick like a balance, the balloons will weigh the same. But if you let air out of one balloon, the balance will tip toward the balloon full of air—because air has weight. Try it!

23

All this air moving from one pressure system to another can mean only one thing—wind! Wind is air in motion. When one mass of air rises or falls, the space it leaves behind can't stay empty. Another mass of air rushes in to fill it. This movement of air is what we feel as wind.

When the sun is shining, the air above land gets heated up faster than the air above the ocean. When warm air from over the land rises, cooler air from above the water fills in the space left behind. These are the sea breezes that feel so good on a hot summer afternoon at the beach!

WARM AIR RISING

COOL SEA BREEZE

WARM LAND

COOL SEA

"HIGH" THERE, PRESSURE!

If you hear a meteorologist say an area of high pressure is coming your way, you can leave your rain jacket at home. High-pressure systems form when a pocket of air is cooler than the rest of the air around it. When air cools, its molecules huddle closer together. This makes the air denser, and it shrinks.

When a pocket of air shrinks, the space around it gets filled by more air. As air moves in to fill the space, it presses down toward the surface of the earth, where you are. The force of the air rushing in breaks up clouds and you get clear, sunny days. That's why high-pressure systems are also called "fair weather systems."

··· DID YOU KNOW? ·········

You can remember the impact of high and low pressure by looking at the symbols on a weather map: The "H" for high pressure means there will be "happy weather," and the L for low pressure means there will be "lousy weather."

BAROMETRIC PRESSURE

Scientists use barometers to measure the amount of pressure in the air. All barometers work pretty much the same way. A long, glass tube is placed with one end in a cup of liquid metal, such as mercury. When air presses down on the liquid in the cup, some of it gets forced up into the tube. The higher the air pressure, the higher the liquid rises in the tube. You can look at a barometer to see if the air pressure is high or low and to track whether air pressure is rising or falling.

WEATHER AND CLIMATE!

THE LOW DOWN ON LOW PRESSURE

A low-pressure system is a whirling mass of warm, moist air. Remember, warm air rises. The air that moves in to fill the space left behind is moving up and away from the earth's surface, not pressing down. So, the air pressure is low and it's time to grab that rain jacket! Here's why.

The higher that mass of warm air rises, the more it thins. As air gets thinner, it can't hold as much heat. It starts to cool by letting out moisture. This creates clouds, precipitation, and bad weather, such as tropical storms and hurricanes. When meteorologists see a low-pressure system, they know people in that area will need their rain gear.

···· DID YOU KNOW? ·······

Your whole body is experiencing about 15 pounds of pressure per square inch. You don't feel it because you have pressure coming from inside your body that balances the pressure from the outside.

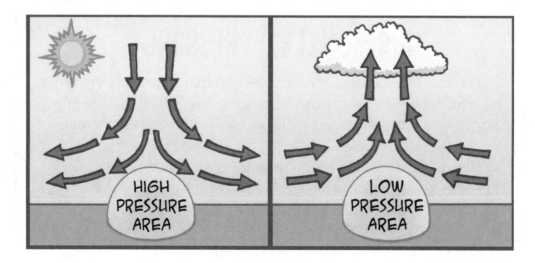

When warm air and cold air meet, they create a front. When you see a weather map on TV, it's usually covered with lines and symbols showing different kinds of fronts. Anywhere you see a front, there will be precipitation. If warm air moves in to meet up with cold air, it rises over the cold air and starts to cool down. If cold air moves in to meet up with warm air, it pushes up the warm air. You know what happens when warm air rises—stormy weather!

Front Symbol	What it means
Cold	A cold front means a cold air mass is moving in the direction of the triangles. As it moves in, the temperature drops and there's a chance of rain.
Warm	A warm front means a warm air mass is moving in the direction of the semi-circles. As it moves in, it will get warmer and it may rain.
Stationary	Cold and warm air masses aren't always strong enough to move each other. A front can stay in the same place for days. This is called a **stationary** front. Cold air is on the semi-circle side trying to push to the other side, and warm air is stuck on the triangle side. Clouds and precipitation are likely.
Occluded	An **occluded** front means a fast-moving front has caught up to a slower-moving front. You'll feel wind and a quick change in temperature.

HIGH ON A MOUNTAINTOP

Temperature change isn't the only thing that affects air pressure. So does altitude. There's far less air pressure on top of a mountain than down by the sea. Why? The lower you are, the more air is above you. Remember, air has weight and presses down on you. But if you go higher up, less air is above you pressing down. Do you know what less air pressure would mean for you if you tried to climb Mount Everest? When air pressure is low, the molecules in the air are more spread out. And what kinds of molecules are in the air? The oxygen molecules you need to breathe! With each breath you take, you get less oxygen because the oxygen molecules are all spread out. If you climb slowly, your body can adjust to the lower air pressure. Your heart will beat faster, your breathing will be faster, and your body will make more of the red blood cells it needs to carry oxygen around your body. If you climb too high, too fast, you can feel sick and get headaches. This is known as altitude sickness. Most people use tanks with extra oxygen in them when they climb to high places.

THIS PERSON IS USING AN OXYGEN TANK WHILE CLIMBING MOUNT EVEREST.
MÁRIO SIMOES (CC BY 2.0)

So, about that rain jacket—how do you know you won't need a winter coat for snow? In the next chapter, we'll learn more about the different types of precipitation!

? CONSIDER AND DISCUSS

It's time to consider and discuss: How does air pressure affect the weather?

PROJECT!

AIR PRESSURE

Experiment with the power of air pressure!

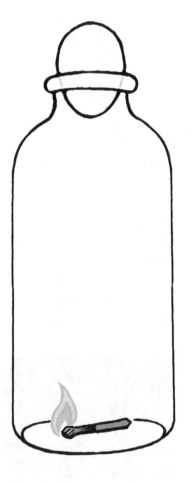

SUPPLIES

* hard-boiled egg
* glass bottle with a wide neck, such as an old-fashioned milk bottle
* match
* science journal and pencil

1 Peel the shell off the hard-boiled egg.

2 Have an adult light a match and then toss it inside the bottle. As soon as the match is in, quickly set the small end of the egg down on the mouth of the bottle.

3 What happens? Write or draw what you see in your science journal.

THINK ABOUT IT: Because the flame from the match uses up some of the air inside the bottle, the air pressure in the bottle gets lower. Meanwhile, the air outside the bottle has a higher pressure. Remember, air pressure tries to balance itself out. The higher pressure air tries to move into the area of lower pressure. If this were a weather system, would precipitation be likely in the bottle or not?

PROJECT!

WARM THE AIR

In this activity watch how air rises and expands when it warms up.

SUPPLIES

* empty plastic bottle
* balloon
* water
* pot big enough to fit the bottle lying down
* science journal and pencil

1 Stretch the balloon over the mouth of the bottle. Set aside.

2 Fill the pot half full of water.

3 Have an adult heat the water until it's very hot but not boiling. Remove the pot from stove.

4 Carefully put the bottle into the hot water (have an adult hold it in if necessary). Wait a little while. What happens to the balloon? Why? Record your observations in your science journal.

THINK ABOUT IT: As the air inside the bottle heats up, the air molecules start moving faster and spreading farther apart. As they expand, the air molecules move out of the bottle and into the balloon. It's still the same amount of air that you started with, but now it's taking up more space.

PROJECT!

MAKE A BAROMETER

Barometers measure the air pressure around you. Make your own barometer so you can keep track of the air pressure and see what kind of weather it brings.

1 Stretch out the balloon by inflating and deflating it a few times. Cut off the neck of the balloon. Pull the balloon tightly over the mouth of the jar and hold it in place with the rubber band.

2 Tape one end of the straw on top of the balloon so that the other end sticks out one side.

3 Take the jar outside and put it up against a wall in a protected area. Tape the paper to the wall and mark where the straw points, your starting point.

4 Every day, check where the straw is pointing. When it moves up or down, mark those places on the paper, labeling them "high" (when it's above the original mark) or "low" (when it's below it). Use what you know about air pressure to explain why.

SUPPLIES

* balloon
* scissors
* glass jar
* rubber band
* straw
* tape
* paper
* marker
* science journal and pencil

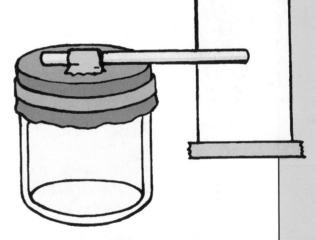

TRY THIS! For a week, record the air pressure in your science journal every day and predict the weather. Then, record the actual weather. How often were your predictions correct?

MAKE AN ANEMOMETER

Anemometers measure wind speed. In this activity, you'll make your own anemometer to put outside to track the wind.

1 Use a marker to color one of your paper cups a bright color. Using the paper punch, poke one hole in four of the paper cups, about ½ inch below the rim. On the fifth cup, punch four equally spaced holes about ¼ inch below the rim. Then, poke another hole in the center of the bottom of the fifth cup with the scissors. This last hole needs to be big enough to fit the pencil and allow the cup to spin on the pencil.

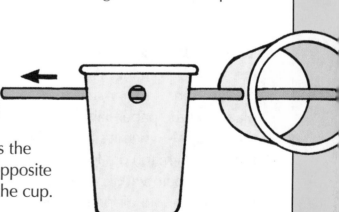

2 Push a straw through the hole from the outside into one of the four cups until it touches the other side of the cup. Fold some of the straw over inside the cup and staple it in place on the far side of the cup. Take the second straw and do the same thing in a second cup.

3 Slide the free end of one of the straws through two opposite holes in the fifth cup. Then, connect one of the remaining cups onto the same straw. Slide it onto the straw until the straw hits the far side. Make sure the cups face opposite directions. Staple the straw inside the cup.

4 Repeat with the last two cups. Slide the free end of the straw stapled into a cup through opposite holes in the fifth cup. Then, slide it through the last empty cup. With the outside cups facing opposite directions, staple the straw to the last cup.

5 Push the pin through the two straws where they cross over each other. Push the pencil, eraser end first, through the bottom hole in the center cup.

6 Push the pin into the eraser as far as it will go.

7 Your anemometer is ready! Push the pencil into the ground in an area where the cups can spin freely without hitting anything. When the wind blows, it will spin your cups. The stronger the wind, the faster your anemometer will spin. Count the number of **rotations** to measure the wind speed! Do you see why one of your cups is a different color?

TRY THIS! If you want your anemometer higher up off the ground, push the pencil into a pot or bowl full of potting soil. You can then move your anemometer easily to catch the best wind.

WORDS to KNOW

rotation: turning around a fixed point.

33

PROJECT!

MAKE A WINDSOCK

A windsock is another instrument for measuring the wind. A windsock shows the direction the wind is coming from. In this project, you'll make your own windsock to hang outside.

1 With an adult's help, bend the coat hanger into a circle the same size as the opening of the sleeve. Using the needle and thread, stitch the wire into the sleeve opening, so it's holding the sleeve open in a circle at one end.

2 Stitch the small rock or weight near the opening of the sleeve. This will give your windsock a little weight, so it keeps facing the wind.

3 Sew each piece of string evenly spaced around the opening in the windsock. Tie the other end of each string to the top of the dowel.

4 Stick the end of the dowel into the ground. When the wind blows, your windsock will puff up and show you which direction the wind is coming from. Use a compass to find out which direction is which, so next time you'll be able to tell just by looking at your windsock.

TRY THIS! On a windy day, think about how the weather was the day before. Can you tell based on the wind direction of your windsock what the weather will be like tomorrow?

CHAPTER 3

PREPARE FOR PRECIPITATION

Can you believe the rain that falls today is the same rain that fell on the *Tyrannosaurus rex* back in the days of the dinosaurs? That's because all the water on Earth is constantly recycling. This includes the water in oceans and rivers and even water locked in glaciers.

The water we have now is all the water we'll ever have. Water never goes away—but it does change form. Water changes from a liquid to a gas and back again, over and over and over. These changes are all part of the water cycle.

? **INVESTIGATE!**

Why is the water cycle so important to life on Earth?

WEATHER AND CLIMATE!

When water is heated by the sun, it evaporates. It turns from a liquid into a gas—called water vapor—and disappears into the air. Water vapor is invisible, but it's all around you! The amount of water vapor, or humidity, in the air changes all the time.

When the air has very little water vapor, the air feels dry. When there is a lot of water vapor in the air, it feels sticky. Sometimes, the air has so much water vapor that you get wet—because it's raining!

ON HUMID DAYS, YOU MIGHT FIND YOURSELF WALKING THROUGH FOG!

Rain happens when water vapor rises high into the atmosphere. Because it's cold up there, the water vapor starts to change back into water. It condenses and sticks together, forming water drops or ice crystals. This makes the water visible again—as clouds!

The drops in the clouds get bigger until they're too heavy to stay in the air. Then, gravity pulls them toward the earth as precipitation, such as rain or snow. The precipitation collects in oceans, rivers, or lakes, or soaks into the ground.

PS Raindrops aren't really tear-shaped, like you see in drawings. They're shaped more like spheres. Sometimes, big raindrops can look a little flattened—like hamburger buns! **Take a look in this video.**

ρ NASA RAINDROP SHAPE VIDEO

SNOW

Do you love the first snowfall each year? Some snow is wet and sticky, perfect for packing snowballs or making snowmen. Some snow is light and fluffy, easy to shovel from the sidewalk. Sometimes, a hard, crusty surface covers softer snow underneath. If the crust is thick enough, you can walk right on top of the snow.

DID YOU KNOW?

The largest snowflake ever recorded was in Montana back in 1887. It was a whopping 15 inches across. Try catching that on your tongue!

The type of snow that falls depends on the layers of warm and cold air that it passes through on the way to the ground.

THE BEAUTY OF SNOWFLAKES

A snowflake starts out high in the atmosphere as a tiny ice crystal. Then, droplets of moisture in the air begin sticking to the crystal and freezing together. As more droplets stick to the crystal, it gets bigger and freezes into wonderful shapes. Most snowflakes have six main arms, and the patterns that form within the crystal are often very complex—and beautiful. Two snowflakes are unlikely to ever have the exact same pattern!

When the crystals get heavy enough, they begin falling toward the ground, and you've got snow!

SLEET? FREEZING RAIN? HAIL?

The most common types of precipitation are rain and snow. It's easy to tell them apart. But what about sleet, freezing rain, and hail? It's not so easy to tell them apart!

sleet: ice pellets, often mixed with rain and snow, that bounce off the ground.

freezing rain: rain that freezes on impact with surfaces, such as roads, cars, and the roofs of buildings.

hail: pellets of frozen rain.

WORDS ⊙ KNOW

Sleet looks a bit like snow, but the little white pellets bounce off the ground when they land. Sleet begins as frozen precipitation very high in the atmosphere. Then, it falls through a layer of warmer air, where it melts. But before sleet hits the ground, it passes through a last layer of thick, cold air, where the pellets freeze again. Because they turn to liquid and then refreeze, they are not light and fluffy.

Freezing rain begins just like sleet does. The difference is the thickness of the last layer of cold air. If it's too thin for the precipitation to freeze, it stays as rain that is very cold. It only freezes when it hits something.

HOW DOES THE RAIN TIE ITS SHOES?

With a rainbow!

Freezing rain doesn't bounce off the ground or cars—it lands and forms a layer of ice. Ice is heavy, and if enough of it forms on trees, they come crashing down—often taking down power lines with them. Freezing rain can cause a lot of damage!

HAIL CAN GET VERY LARGE

Hail can look like small golf balls. This precipitation begins as tiny clumps of ice in thunderclouds. But these clumps of ice don't just fall to the ground. First, they go through quite a bumpy ride inside a thundercloud! Wind moves them up and down, through layers of cool air and warm air.

When the clumps of ice pass through warm air, raindrops attach to them. Then, when the wind catches them and lifts them up again through the cool air, they freeze.

DID YOU KNOW?

The largest hailstone in recorded history was found in South Dakota in 2010. It was 8 inches across, about as big as a soccer ball. And it was found after it had already melted a little!

This happens again and again, and the ice clumps get bigger and bigger—until they're hailstones. When the hailstones get too heavy, the wind can't carry them up again and they fall to the ground. Hailstones can get large enough to damage property.

> **drought:** a long period of little or no rain.
>
> **decade:** a 10-year period of time.
>
> **food chain:** a community of animals and plants where each different plant or animal is eaten by another plant or animal higher up in the chain.
>
> **WORDS ⊚ KNOW**

DESERTS AND RAINFORESTS

Some areas—such as deserts—are used to little or no rain. The animals and plants that live in these places have adapted to dry conditions that can often be extreme.

DRY AS DROUGHT

Usually, high-pressure and low-pressure systems pass over an area and move on. Sometimes, though, a high-pressure system gets stuck and the air is only being pushed down and not up.

If air doesn't rise, it doesn't rain. This means nice, dry, sunny weather for days. But if it lasts a few weeks or years, it becomes a **drought**. Sometimes, droughts even last a **decade** or more. Drought threatens plants, animals, and people, who all depend on the rain. After all, plants are the beginning of the **food chain**, so it's important that they have enough water to grow—without plants, nothing can survive.

(PS) **Watch this video and learn about the link between humans and drought.**

🔍 NAT GEO DROUGHT ────→

WEATHER AND CLIMATE!

The camel is an animal that is well adapted to living in the desert. You may have heard that camels store water in the humps on their backs. That's not really true. A camel's hump stores fat deposits that the camel can use for energy, so they can go for long periods of time without needing water. And camels can live with much higher temperatures than many other animals. They also have huge, wide feet to help them walk on the sand easily and long eyelashes to protect their eyes from blowing sand. They can even close their nostrils!

But put that camel in the rainforest, and it would struggle to survive. However, the sloth is an animal that's well adapted to live high in the canopy of the rainforest. For example, its hair grows backward, from its stomach toward its back, to help the rain run off easily as the sloth hangs from its claws.

MOUNTAIN CLIMATE

Because it gets colder the higher you go, the climate at the bottom of a big mountain is very different from the climate at the top. Even when the distance from the bottom of a mountain to the top isn't that great, the ecosystem can change dramatically as you go up.

You might find a steamy jungle environment at the base of a mountain and icy, snow-capped peaks at the top. Plants and animals that live at the bottom often can't survive higher up.

The climate on different sides of a mountain can be dramatically different as well. This is because the sheer size of mountains affects the weather.

When air moves over oceans and lakes, it picks up moisture evaporating from the water. When the air moves over the land and hits a mountain, the wind lifts and rises over the mountain. As air rises up one side of the mountain, it thins and cools. When it cools, that side of the mountain—called the windward side—gets rain.

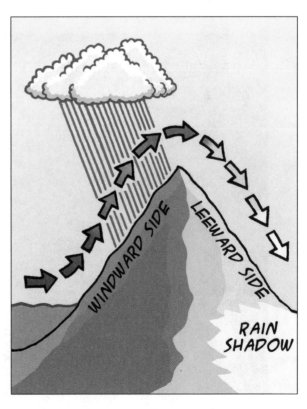

WINDWARD SIDE

LEEWARD SIDE

RAIN SHADOW

leeward side: the side of a mountain that doesn't get hit by the traveling winds.

rain shadow: an area beside a mountain that gets little or no rain because it all fell on the mountain itself.

WORDS to KNOW

··· **DID YOU KNOW?** ····

Some plants and animals live only in specific rain shadows. The Devils Hole pupfish, for example, is a tiny fish that only lives in the shallow pools of Death Valley.

By the time the clouds make it over the mountain, they've lost all their moisture and dried out. The non-windy side—called the leeward side—of the mountain can be incredibly dry.

When an area that extends from the leeward side of a mountain doesn't get any rain, it's said to be in the rain shadow of the mountain. Sometimes, these areas get so dry that they become deserts. The Gobi Desert formed because it's on the leeward side of the Himalayas in Asia.

THE DRY GOBI DESERT

THE RAINBOW CONNECTION

Have you ever seen a rainbow? How about a double rainbow? You usually only see a rainbow after it rains. That's because rainbows are created when sunlight hits raindrops that are still suspended in the air. To see a rainbow, you must have the sun behind you and the raindrops in front of you.

Light is made up of different colors, although you don't usually see all these colors at the same time. But in a rainbow, light is split into its different colors and you can see them all at once! The colors of a rainbow are always in the same pattern: red, orange, yellow, green, blue, indigo, and violet.

When there is a double rainbow, the second one is above and outside the first one. Its colors are the same but in reversed order. Red is on the inside at the bottom and violet is on the outside at the top.

CREDIT: SHEILA SUND (CC BY 2.0)

We've learned about how clouds are formed and the role they play in forming precipitation. In the next chapter, we'll take a closer look at what different clouds mean for different types of weather.

? CONSIDER AND DISCUSS

It's time to consider and discuss: Why is the water cycle so important to life on Earth?

SUPPLIES

* clear bottle or jar with straight sides
* ruler
* permanent marker
* science journal and pencil

MAKE A RAIN GAUGE

How do meteorologists know how much rain has fallen? They use a rain gauge. Make your own rain gauge so you can track the rainfall you receive at your house.

1 Remove any labels from the bottle or jar and make sure it is clean and dry.

2 Place the ruler against the jar. Using the marker, start at the bottom of your jar and measure up from the bottom, marking and labeling every quarter inch.

3 Set your rain gauge outside where nothing is hanging over it to block the rain. If you think your gauge might tip over, bury it slightly in the ground or brace it with stones or bricks on all sides.

4 Check your gauge after each rain. Record the results in your science journal. Be sure to empty your gauge after every rainfall so you can get an accurate reading for the next one.

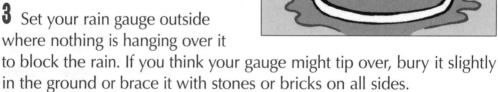

THINK ABOUT IT: Why would your gauge report different results than what you might hear from the weather forecaster on your local news station?

46

PROJECT!

MAKE A SNOWFLAKE

Make a permanent snowflake to remind you of winter year-round! Hang it near a window to make it sparkle.

Caution: An adult must help with the boiling water.

1 Cut a pipe cleaner into three equal pieces. Twist them together in the middle and spread out the ends to form your snowflake shape. Make sure your snowflake is small enough that it easily fits in the jar.

2 Cut a piece of string. Tie one end to your snowflake and the other to your pencil. The string needs to be long enough for the snowflake to hang from the pencil inside the jar, but don't let the snowflake touch the bottom of the jar. Adjust the string until it's the right length. Put the snowflake aside for now.

3 Mix the borax with the boiling water, using three tablespoons of borax for every cup of water. Stir really well. Stir the food coloring into the water if you want. Once the mixture has cooled a bit, pour it into the jar.

4 Hang your snowflake in the jar and leave it there overnight. In the morning, the snowflake will be covered with crystals. Hang it in a window where it catches the light.

SUPPLIES

* pipe cleaners
* scissors
* wide-mouth glass jar
* string
* pencil
* borax from the laundry detergent section of the store— look for "20 Mule Team Borax Laundry Booster" (you can use salt or sugar, but it takes longer)
* boiling water
* blue food coloring (optional)

THINK ABOUT IT:

How does changing the shape of your pipe cleaner change the growth of the crystals? Do you think that is how snowflakes all have different shapes, too? What makes each snowflake different?

SUPPLIES

* ✳ glass jar
* ✳ hot water—NOT boiling
* ✳ plate
* ✳ ice cubes
* ✳ science journal and pencil

MAKE IT RAIN

In this activity, you can see how rain forms in the atmosphere.

Caution: Have an adult help with the hot water.

1 Remove any labels from your jar so that you have a clear view.

2 Have an adult warm up enough water to pour several inches into the glass jar. Be sure it's not boiling water, or the jar will break.

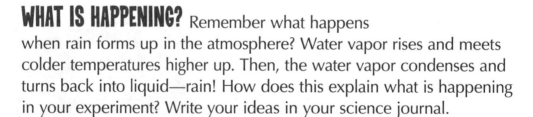

3 Place the plate on top of the jar to seal it. Put the ice cubes on top of the plate and wait for several minutes. What happens?

WHAT IS HAPPENING? Remember what happens when rain forms up in the atmosphere? Water vapor rises and meets colder temperatures higher up. Then, the water vapor condenses and turns back into liquid—rain! How does this explain what is happening in your experiment? Write your ideas in your science journal.

THINK ABOUT IT: Can you think of anything that would make your "rain" form faster? How about slower?

PROJECT!

MAKE A RAINBOW

SUPPLIES

* drinking glass
* water
* sunny day or flashlight
* white paper

If you want to see a rainbow, you don't have to wait for one to appear outside. You can make your own rainbow—inside!

1 Fill the glass with water until it's about three-quarters full.

2 Stand next to a window through which the sun is shining. You can also use a flashlight.

3 Hold the white paper on the other side of the glass and let the light shine through the water. The water will break up the light into all its colors and a rainbow will form on your paper! Experiment with different angles for the water and light to see what effect that has on your rainbow.

THINK ABOUT IT: Why do you think a rainbow forms in the shape it does instead of, for example, a straight line?

PROJECT!

MAKE A RAIN STICK

Do you like the sound of rain? You can make a rain stick to listen to rain any time—without getting wet!

1 A spiral seam runs the length of the cardboard tube. Using the marker, make dots about a half-inch apart all the way down the tube, just about a half-inch inch above this seam. This is where you will put the nails. If you put the nails right on the seam, the tube can split.

2 With an adult's help, carefully poke a nail into each dot and push it in. The nail should not go all the way through to the other side of the tube.

3 Run a piece of duct tape around and around the tube, covering the nail heads and holding them in place.

4 Cut a piece of paper large enough to cover the openings on the ends of the tube. Cover one end and tape the paper in place.

SUPPLIES

* long cardboard tube (wrapping-paper tubes are the best, but you can use a paper towel tube, or even duct tape several paper towel tubes together)

* marker

* several 1-inch nails

* duct tape

* heavy colored paper

* dry rice and/or dry beans

* stickers

5 Pour about a handful of dry rice or beans in the open end. You can use a little of both. For now, cover the open end with your hand and turn the rain stick over to hear the sound. If you want more noise, add more beans or rice. When you have the sound you want, use the other piece of paper to cover the open end of the tube and tape it closed.

6 Decorate the tube with markers, stickers, or colored paper. To hear the rain, just turn your rain stick over from end to end!

DID YOU KNOW?

No one knows where rain sticks originated or what they were used for. Some people think they came from early communities in Africa or Mesoamerica. Perhaps people believed they could bring rain during dry times. Maybe they were simply an early musical instrument. Researchers have found no evidence about where rain sticks came from!

TRY THIS! Can you make your rain stick make different noises? How?

THE SOUND OF RAIN

Many people find the sound of falling rain soothing. Scientists have actually studied the sound of rain and can use the sound to measure the size and number of raindrops that are falling! When rain hits the ocean, there is a sound of a sharp impact, followed by a "fizzing" sound. That's because the impact on the water makes tiny bubbles rise up. Scientists can use those sounds to determine rainfall at sea.

CHAPTER 4

COUNTING ON CLOUDS

Like rainbows, clouds can be fun to look at. They are always moving and changing. Try lying on your back and watching clouds. They can form into any shape that your imagination can dream up!

Not all clouds are great for daydreaming, though. Some clouds carry dangerous lightning. Others might carry hail. But they all carry a message, and you can figure out how to read those messages by learning "cloud language."

 INVESTIGATE!

What can clouds tell you about the weather?

For example, a wispy, light cloud high up in the sky is telling you that the weather is going to be great today. But a tall, thick cloud is warning you that a storm is coming.

··· DID YOU KNOW? ·····

Other planets have clouds, too. Venus has lots of clouds. But those clouds are made up of poisonous gases. No cloud-gazing there!

WHAT IS A CLOUD?

As we've learned, clouds are made up of water—water vapor and ice crystals to be exact. When water vapor rises into the air, it starts getting cooler and condensing back into a liquid, or water droplets. These droplets begin to cling to tiny dust specks that are floating around in the sky. Soon, more and more droplets form. When several billion of these droplets exist, you can see them in the sky—as a cloud!

WORDS ⊚ KNOW

nimbus: a large, gray rain cloud.

cirrus: a high-altitude cloud characterized by wispy strands.

stratus: gray clouds that often cover the whole sky.

cumulus: a low-level, fluffy-looking cloud.

WORDS ⊚ KNOW

Learn about how clouds affect climate.

🔍 CLIMATE KIDS CLOUD CLIMATE

Clouds are white because they're reflecting all the colors in the light from the sun. When clouds get dense with water droplets, all the light can't get through and they turn gray, or almost black. That usually means they're getting ready to drop their water down on you!

CLOUD "LANGUAGE"

These are the types of clouds you probably see a lot. There are many other types, too. A **nimbus** cloud, which has rain or snow already falling, means thunder and lightning could be coming soon!

Type of cloud	What it means
Thin, wispy clouds like streamers that are high in the sky are **cirrus** clouds.	The weather is nice, but a change in the weather is coming within 24 hours.
Gray clouds that often cover the whole sky—like fog that doesn't reach the ground—are **stratus** clouds.	It's probably already misting or drizzling.
White, fluffy clouds that look like cotton are **cumulus** clouds.	Good weather—usually.

There are many kinds of clouds—and each has its own name. Cirrus, stratus, and cumulus are common types of clouds. Each cloud looks different and tells us something about the weather.

FOG

Have you ever gotten up in the morning and looked outside—only to see cloudy whiteness covering everything? You're looking at fog.

⋯ DID YOU KNOW? ⋯

The Grand Banks off the island of Newfoundland, Canada, is the foggiest place on Earth! Here, very cold water from the north meets very warm water from the south.

A FOGGY FOREST CAN LOOK MYSTERIOUS!

WHY SHOULDN'T YOU FIGHT WITH A CLOUD?

He'll storm out on you!

Fog is a giant cloud that forms right near the ground. Different kinds of fog form for different reasons. The kind you see in the morning forms when the ground cools overnight, bringing down the temperature of the air above it. Water vapor cools, condenses around dust, and makes fog.

Another kind of fog forms when warm air moves over a cooler surface. For example, when warm ocean air blows over the cooler beach in the morning, the land cools down the air, creating fog.

Mountains can create fog, too. When warm air slides up the side of a cool mountain, the cooled air causes fog on mountainsides.

Clouds help meteorologists make lots of predictions, and, in the case of extreme weather, some of those predictions are warnings! We'll learn more in the next chapter.

··· DID YOU KNOW? ·······

During fall and winter in California's Central Valley, a kind of fog called tule fog is common. Cold mountain air drops down from the coast and Sierra Nevada Mountains. It gets stuck there for days or weeks. This fog can be so thick that sometimes you can't see farther than a foot in front of you!

? CONSIDER AND DISCUSS

It's time to consider and discuss: What can clouds tell you about the weather?

PROJECT!

MAKE A 3-D CLOUD CHART

SUPPLIES

* book or website with cloud types and pictures
* cotton
* poster board
* white glue
* black marker with a wide tip

Create a 3-D cloud chart to help you remember what different types of clouds mean.

1 Look at the chart on page 54 for information on common types of clouds. Also, check the library or the internet (with an adult's permission) to add other clouds, such as nimbus, altostratus, cumulonimbus, cirrocumulus, altocumulus, and stratocumulus.

(PS) **To learn more about cloud types, check out this website.**

🔍 WEATHER CLOUD CHART →

2 Use the cotton to shape the different cloud types and glue them to your poster board. Label your clouds.

3 To make gray rain clouds or thunderclouds, gently color the cotton with the black marker.

4 Hang up your chart near a window and use it to identify the clouds you see.

THINK ABOUT IT: What kind of cloud do you see most often? Least often?

PROJECT!

SUPPLIES

* 4 egg whites
* mixing bowl and electric mixer
* ½ teaspoon cream of tartar
* 2 cups sugar
* plastic Ziploc bag
* scissors
* cookie sheet

MAKE SOME EDIBLE CLOUDS

Make clouds to eat to share with family and friends. Try to make the treats look like different clouds!

Caution: Ask an adult to help with the oven and the mixer.

1 With an adult's help, preheat the oven to 200 degrees Fahrenheit (about 110 degrees Celsius).

2 Place the egg whites in the mixing bowl. Using an electric mixer, beat the egg whites until they're foamy. Beat in the cream of tartar at medium speed. Then, gradually add 2 tablespoons of sugar.

3 When soft peaks begin to form, add another tablespoon of sugar and turn the mixer up to high speed. When stiff peaks form, gradually add the rest of the sugar while beating.

4 When the mixture is very stiff and shiny, spoon the mixture into your plastic Ziploc bag and snip off one of the corners. Squeeze the bag to squirt some clouds out onto your cookie sheet in the shapes you want.

CLOUDS THEN AND NOW

Have you ever seen photographs of landscapes from long ago? Nowadays, many people have a camera on their phone, but before this century, far fewer photographs were taken, and even fewer were taken in the nineteenth century. Scientists are researching clouds from long ago and how they might have looked different from clouds today. Maybe they formed differently, too. That's because there are materials in the air now that weren't there before the Industrial Revolution, when factories started putting more pollutants and other things into the air. So how do scientists learn what clouds were like long before smartphone cameras? A device at a laboratory called CERN is being used to create different types of clouds. Scientists can produce clouds from the materials that existed in the atmosphere 200 years ago and see what they were like. This is an important part of learning more about **climate change** and what humans can do to help the planet stay as healthy as possible.

5 After you use up all the egg white mixture, bake your clouds for about 1 hour. They should be completely dry to the touch. While you enjoy and share your cloud treat, explain what each one is and the weather it brings.

TRY THIS! How could you make a "storm" cloud?

WORDS ᴛᴏ KNOW

climate change: changes in the earth's climate patterns, including rising temperatures, which is called global warming. Climate change can happen through natural or manmade processes.

IT'S FOGGY!

Watch fog form right in front of you in this activity.

1 Tape the black paper around the back outside of the jar. This will help you see your fog better.

2 Fill the jar about a third of the way with the warm water. Add a few drops of food coloring.

3 Have an adult light the match and hold it over the jar opening for a few seconds. This will warm the air in the jar and produce smoke. Then, have them toss the match into the jar. Cover the top of the jar with the bag of ice.

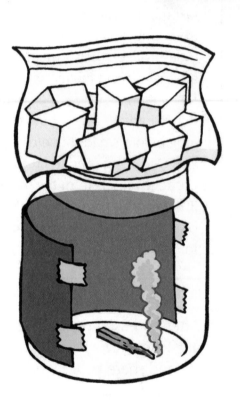

4 What happens inside the jar? As the warm water begins to evaporate, the water vapor clings to the smoke particles from the match, just like they cling to dust high in the atmosphere. As the air cools down from the ice, the vapor begins condensing. You've made your own fog! Record your observations in your science journal.

THINK ABOUT IT: How thick can you grow your "fog"?

CHAPTER 5

ARE YOU READY FOR EXTREME WEATHER?

Our weather is either sunny, cloudy, or a combination of both. Sometimes, it rains or maybe it snows a little bit. No big deal, right? But sometimes, the weather can get downright dangerous. There might be massive thunderstorms, a blizzard, or even a hurricane or tornado.

Extreme weather happens all across the world. However, some areas experience more extreme weather than others. For example, the center region of the United States is often called "Tornado Alley." That's because it gets more tornadoes than other parts of the country—a lot more.

? INVESTIGATE!

What are some ways you can protect yourself from extreme weather?

THUNDERSTORMS

You probably know what thunderstorms sound like, but do you know what causes them? Thunderstorms happen when a cold air mass collides with a warm air mass. When the difference in temperature between the two air masses is big, a storm is likely to happen.

When the cold air mass hits the warm air mass, it rushes underneath the warm mass. That pushes the warm air mass up at a sharp angle into the atmosphere. As the warm air mass hits the higher—and colder—air in the atmosphere, all the moisture it's carrying quickly condenses. The result is a dark storm cloud full of lightning and thunder.

CREDIT: SENIOR AIRMAN JUSTIN ARMSTRONG

Lightning is a bright flash of electricity that builds up during a thunderstorm. Think about what happens when you rub your feet on the carpet and then touch something. Zap! First, you built up an electrical charge, and then, you released it. Lightning is just like that, but on a much bigger scale.

Lightning is created when some of the water droplets in the storm cloud turn to ice and start bumping into each

You can see a detailed explanation of how lightning forms.

— — — — — — →

🔍 LIGHTNING WEATHER WIZ

other. As the ice particles collide and rub against each other, an electrical charge starts building up inside the cloud.

At the same time, a charge is building up on the ground under the cloud. The charge is strongest around anything that sticks up—mountains, trees, even grass. The charge coming down from the cloud connects with the charge coming up from the ground—zap! You've got lightning!

THUNDERSNOW

You don't usually hear thunder in winter, but a heavy snowstorm can include lightning. And when there's lightning, there's thunder! This is called thundersnow. Thundersnow can only happen if the air has a lot of moisture. Most thundersnow happens near large lakes, such as the Great Salt Lake in Utah or any of the Great Lakes along the border of the United States and Canada.

Part of staying safe in a lightning storm is making sure you aren't the tallest thing in your immediate area. Also, avoid any tall structures that will attract that electricity.

You hear thunder because the air near the lightning heats up quickly and expands. This generates a **sound wave**, which causes the loud booming sound we call thunder.

TORNADOES

A tornado is nature's most violent storm. You probably know about the "twister" shape of a tornado. These spinning columns of air start from powerful thunderstorms called **supercells** that go all the way down to the ground. The strongest tornado winds swirl up to 300 miles per hour, destroying large buildings and trees in seconds.

Have you ever seen a tornado? Close to 1,000 tornadoes occur in the United States every year. This is more than anywhere else in the world. Most of these storms happen in Tornado Alley, an area between Texas and South Dakota.

In the spring and summer, warm and wet air from the Gulf of Mexico rises to meet cool and dry air coming down from Canada. The Canadian winds high in the atmosphere blow at a different speed than Gulf winds lower down. When they collide, they can create a spinning storm.

CREDIT: LANE PEARMAN (CC BY 2.0)

 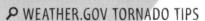

Want to know what to do to stay safe in a tornado? **Check out this video.**

🔍 WEATHER.GOV TORNADO TIPS

If the winds are lined up just right and are strong enough, the storm spins like a top and makes a cloud shaped like a funnel. When rain and hail fall from the storm, the funnel drops until it touches ground. It's time to take shelter because a tornado has landed!

HURRICANES

Hurricanes are massive tropical storms that form over warm ocean water. The warm, moist air rises upward, and air from the surrounding area swirls into the space left by the rising air. Then, that air is warmed by the ocean. The cycle continues, growing into a powerful, spiraling windstorm.

WEATHER AND CLIMATE!

As the storm begins to spin faster and faster, an "eye" forms in the very center. The eye is calm and clear. People who experience the eye of a hurricane often think the hurricane is over—but there's a whole second part to come!

Hurricanes don't stay together very well once they hit land. But their heavy rains, strong winds, and large waves can do a lot of damage to buildings, trees, and cars in coastal areas. Unlike tornadoes, hurricanes can last for a while.

··· DID YOU KNOW? ··

Hurricane Katrina devastated New Orleans, Louisiana, in August 2005. It was the third deadliest hurricane in United States history, with 1,836 people dead from the storm.

To help scientists keep track of them, hurricanes are given names. The names go in alphabetical order, alternating between male and female names. At the beginning of each hurricane season, names restart again from the letter A. If a storm turns out to be devastating or deadly, that name is never used again. Hurricane Sandy in 2012 was so bad that the name Sandy has been retired.

A HURRICANE FROM FAR ABOVE. CAN YOU SPOT THE EYE?

Each season has about five or six named hurricanes. The official hurricane season is from June 1 to November 30, when most, but not all, hurricanes happen.

TOOLS OF THE WEATHER TRADE

Weather satellites and Doppler radar help meteorologists spot weather that's on the way. Normal radar works by sending out a signal that bounces off an object and returns. It shows that something is there—but it's often hard to know what that something is.

Doppler radar also sends out a signal that returns, but it can measure wind speed, type of precipitation, and even the size of hail. Doppler radar can tell meteorologists whether an object is getting closer or moving farther away.

Weather forecasts are not always perfect, but as technology improves, forecasts are better all the time. Today, forecasts are usually accurate up to about five days in advance.

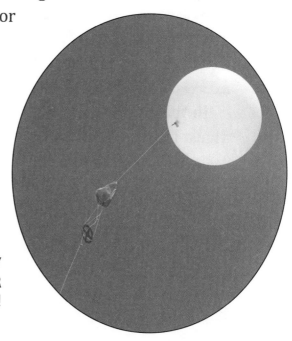

ONE WAY METEOROLOGISTS STUDY WEATHER IS BY SENDING WEATHER BALLOONS INTO THE ATMOSPHERE!
CREDIT: COD NEWSROOM (CC BY 2.0)

weather satellite: a small electronic object that circles the earth and sends back pictures of weather patterns.

Doppler radar: an instrument that uses signals to measure an object, such as a storm, in motion.

radar: a system that sends out pulses of radio waves that reflect back.

technology: tools, methods, and systems used to solve a problem or do work.

WORDS TO KNOW

THE POWER OF A CATEGORY 1

On September 14, 2018, Hurricane Florence made landfall just south of Wrightsville Beach, North Carolina. Although it was a Category 1 hurricane (Category 5 is the strongest hurricane) it was the wettest storm recorded in the Carolinas, dropping almost 36 inches of rain. The storm stalled, causing widespread flooding and damage as far inland as Chapel Hill, causing major rivers to spill over their banks. The city of Wilmington was cut off from the rest of the state because of the floodwaters, and 54 deaths were attributed to the storm.

DID YOU KNOW?

Hurricane hunters are people who fly special planes right up to and into the hurricane to take measurements and report back about the conditions. Would you like this job?

Some of the things weather forecasters try to predict include temperature, precipitation, and air pressure. They also try to make sure people know about any extreme weather heading their way. Sometimes, warnings about weather can be the difference between life and death.

In this book so far, we have talked a lot about weather. What about the climate? How is the climate changing and what does that have to do with humans? We'll explore this topic next!

? CONSIDER AND DISCUSS

It's time to consider and discuss: What are some ways you can protect yourself from extreme weather?

PROJECT!

LIGHTNING!

You can't make real lightning, of course, but this activity will show you how everything carries an electrical charge and how lightning really does happen.

SUPPLIES

* disposable foil pie pan
* pencil with full eraser
* tack
* foam plate
* piece of wool fabric

1 Turn the foil pie pan upside down. Hold the pencil on the pan with the eraser down. Push the tack through the center of the pie pan from underneath into the eraser.

2 Put the foam plate upside down on a table. Trying not to handle the plate, quickly rub the bottom with wool fabric for a few minutes.

ZAP!

3 Pick up the foil pie pan using the pencil as a handle. Place it on top of the foam plate. Then, touch the pie pan with your finger. You should feel a small shock! If not, rub the foam plate again, but longer. If you do this in the dark, you'll even see a little spark.

THINK ABOUT IT: Like real lightning, it's all about the charges of electricity. The charges on the pie pan come from the wool-rubbed foam plate. They jump to the charges on your finger, just like a teeny tiny lightning bolt. How far away can you move your finger and still make the little spark jump across to meet it?

PROJECT!

MAKE A WEATHER STATION

Make your own weather station using some of the other projects in this book.

1 Attach the dowels to the back of the pegboard using pipe cleaners, twisting them tightly. Let the dowels extend about a foot past the base of the pegboard. You'll use these to stick the weather station into the ground.

2 Using the pegboard as a base, attach the weather instruments (the other projects you've made from this book) with the pipe cleaners. Make sure nothing is blocking anything else. You want your barometer straw to move freely, for example. And you want the rain gauge to have a clear opening to the sky. The wind sock should be able to blow in any direction.

3 Set your weather station outside where it won't get bumped. Push the dowels into the ground so the weather station is upright and stable. Check the weather instruments every day to make sure everything is working properly.

4 Make a chart in your science journal. Columns should include these headings: "Day," "Observation," "Prediction," and "Actual Weather." Record your observations in your science journal each day. How accurate were your predictions?

THINK ABOUT IT: What else could you add to your weather station to make it even more complete?

PROJECT!

MAKE A WEATHER SAFETY KIT

You can't stop bad weather from happening. But you can be prepared for it. Keep your family safe by having this weather safety kit always stocked and ready for anything that comes your way. Keep a weather safety kit in your car, too.

SUPPLIES

* a big, sturdy plastic box with a lid
* assorted emergency items (see step 1 for suggestions)
* paper and pen
* tape

1 Talk with your family about what should be put into the weather safety kit. Some ideas include food and water, blankets, a first-aid kit, flashlights and batteries, a multifunction tool, waterproof matches, plastic bags, tissues or toilet paper, and a battery-powered radio. Energy bars and dried fruit are good food choices because they last a long time. Write down your list. Then, gather everything together and put it in the box.

2 Write down emergency phone numbers on the paper—such as for the electric company, police, fire department, as well as friends and family.

3 Tape your list to the inside of the lid. This way, if you use anything up, you can use it as a checklist to know what to replace.

4 Store your weather safety kit in a safe place, such as a hall closet, where you can get to it easily in case of a storm. You want to be able to locate the box easily in the dark.

THINK ABOUT IT: How often should you stock your kit? Is there anything you should change out, depending on the season?

WEATHER GAME

SUPPLIES

* index cards
* markers, crayons, or colored pencils
* large piece of paper or poster board (or several pieces of paper taped together)
* small figures or drawings to use as playing pieces

The weather may not always be extreme, but it can often affect outdoor activities. Make and play this board game to see how.

1 On several index cards, draw pictures representing a different weather event—sunshine, rain, thunderstorm, snow, wind, extreme weather (such as a tornado or hurricane), cold temperatures, steamy heat, and so on. The more you can think of, the better. Write "Weather Card" on the blank side of each card and set them to one side.

2 Take some more index cards and draw pictures (or write descriptions) of outdoor activities on them. Try to think of as many activities as possible—skiing, swimming, splashing in puddles, flying a kite, catching snowflakes on your tongue, having a picnic, riding your bike, sledding, and so on. Write "Activity Card" on the blank side of each index card.

3 Put the cards aside and get out the paper or poster board. This will be your game board. Make a starting point and an end. Draw a winding path around the board from the start to the end. Then, divide the path into individual squares. You'll move your playing pieces along these squares. You probably don't want too many squares, or the game will take too long.

STAY ALERT

Many times, people underestimate the power of the weather, but it's important that you pay attention and heed warnings from weather experts. Although it's disappointing when outdoor plans are canceled because of the weather, it's far better to be safe and plan your fun for another day. For example, even a few inches of fast-moving water can sweep you off your feet—or float a small car! So, it's best to reschedule if the weather looks bad. You can always stay inside and play this weather game instead!

4 Take the weather cards and place them face down in the middle of the board. Place the activity cards face down in a separate pile.

5 Begin with everyone's playing piece at the start. To play, pick an activity card and a weather card. If the activity is something you could do in those weather conditions, move your piece forward a square. If you can't do the activity in the weather conditions, you don't get to move. Just put the cards down and the next person picks.

6 If you run out of cards, shuffle each deck and keep going through them. The first person to reach the finish wins.

THINK ABOUT IT: How have people created sports and fun things to do in spite of—or because of—the weather? Are there any sports that wouldn't exist without certain weather conditions?

A TORNADO IN A BOTTLE

SUPPLIES

* empty 2-liter plastic bottle with cap
* water
* liquid soap
* vinegar
* glitter and food coloring

Find out how a tornado looks—without having to chase one down!

1 Remove any labels and clean the empty plastic bottle, if necessary.

2 Fill the bottle about three-quarters full of water.

3 Add about a teaspoon each of the liquid soap and the vinegar. Add glitter and food coloring.

4 Screw on the cap tightly and shake the bottle to mix the ingredients.

5 Hold the bottle upside down and swirl it in a circular motion. A funnel-shaped whirlpool will form inside. You've got your own small tornado!

THINK ABOUT IT: Why does the spinning nature of a tornado create so much damage?

CHAPTER 6

CLIMATE CHANGE CHALLENGE

Daily weather forecasts may not be perfect, but you can always have a general idea of what to expect when you step outside. If you live in the northern United States, you know it's going to be cold in the winter. Ponds freeze and it usually snows. Ice skating and sledding are more likely activities than riding your bicycle. And if you're down South in the summer, you expect it to be steaming hot. A swim and a cold glass of lemonade are what you want!

You know this because the climate of an area is pretty steady each year. The temperature ranges of each season are fairly predictable. But what if you look at the big picture—the climate of an area during a very long time, not just one year or even 10 years?

? INVESTIGATE!

Why is climate change a hot topic today?

If you made a giant chart that tracked the weather during hundreds and thousands of years, you might find that the climate of an area varied through time. It might have been colder during the Ice Age around 20,000 years ago. Or it might have been warmer 1,000 years ago, when the earth's climate was wetter and warmer than it is today.

Sometimes, knowing the difference between weather and climate is hard. **Check out this video for some help.**

PS

— — — — — — — →

🔍 CLIMATE WEATHER DOG

Unlike daily weather changes, climate changes happen very, very slowly. Climate change takes place so slowly that scientists must look back at long periods of time to see trends.

HUMANS VS. CLIMATE

Some variation in climate is caused by natural events, such as tiny changes in the earth's orbit or a change in the sun's output of heat. Another cause can be strong eruptions of volcanoes. These can shoot very fine dust high in the atmosphere. The dust particles can weaken the strength of sunlight for months. And that's enough to affect the climate for some time.

DID YOU KNOW?

The average global sea level is expected to rise between seven and 23 inches before the end of this century because of climate change.

However, almost all scientists around the world agree that there's another major reason for climate change—human activity.

Global temperatures are increasing because of how humans live their lives today. When **fossil fuels** such as natural gas and oil are burned to create energy to heat homes and make cars move, they release gases into the atmosphere.

Those gases, including carbon dioxide, form an invisible blanket around the planet. This blanket keeps heat trapped close to the earth and causes the temperature all around the globe to rise very slowly. This is called **global warming**.

fossil fuel: a fuel made from the remains of plants and animals that lived millions of years ago.

global warming: an increase in the average temperature of the earth's atmosphere.

WORDS ᴛᴏ KNOW

(PS) **Find out more climate change at this NASA website.**

— — — — — — — — — — — — →

🔎 NASA KIDS CLIMATE

BURNING COAL RELEASES GREENHOUSE GASES INTO THE AIR.

WEATHER AND CLIMATE!

The gases themselves are called greenhouse gases, because they act just like the glass of a greenhouse. They let sunlight in to warm the earth but stop heat from escaping.

Rising global temperatures mean less rain and more drought. They also mean that glaciers are melting, which causes the levels of the world's oceans to rise. All these changes put animals, plants, and people at risk.

Plus, the planet has only a certain amount of fossil fuels to begin with. Scientists and concerned people are asking everyone to use less of these fossil fuels.

So, what can you do? If you recycle your trash and reuse what you have, you can save fossil fuels. Not only will this preserve what the planet has, but it will also reduce the amount of greenhouse gases going into the atmosphere.

GREENHOUSE GASES TRAP THE SUN'S ENERGY

renewable energy: a form of energy that doesn't get used up, including the energy of the sun and the wind.

WORDS ⊕ KNOW

Another thing you can do is walk, bike, or take public transportation to places instead of driving, whenever possible. Plus, does your family use LED light bulbs? These are the most energy-efficient light bulbs. And don't forget to turn off lights and other electronics whenever you're not using them to conserve resources.

Some families and businesses use renewable energies to fuel activity. Solar, wind, and geothermal energies are all unlimited—we can't run out of them, and using them is a much cleaner process than relying on oil and gas.

THE POWER COUNTY WIND FARM IN IDAHO

STORMS OF THE FUTURE

Scientists believe that storms will become more intense because of climate change. As sea levels rise, flooding will become more regular. Because of the increase in temperature and moisture content of the atmosphere, tropical cyclone rainfall rates will likely increase, too. Some models predict that the maximum intensity of Atlantic hurricanes will increase by about 5 percent.

By slowing global warming, the planet can experience its own natural climate changes during long periods of time.

Weather and climate are among the most powerful natural forces on our planet. While humans are no contest against the strength of Mother Nature, we can be sure that we're prepared and safe by studying the patterns of weather and climate and being ready for any strong or dangerous weather.

But weather isn't all scary! There's a lot of really great things that we can appreciate and enjoy about weather, such as knowing the weather will be perfect for a fall picnic or a beautiful breezy spring day to fly a kite. You can snuggle up with a book and listen to the rainfall or plant a garden, knowing that rain will help make it grow. If we understand weather, we can better appreciate and care for our amazing planet together.

CONSIDER AND DISCUSS

It's time to consider and discuss: Why is climate change a hot topic today?

PROJECT!

GLOBAL WARMING CHECKLIST

We can all do a lot to pitch in and cut back on the use of fossil fuels. Make this checklist for your family so you'll know how you can help.

1 Using the starter list below, write each item on its own line and make a big box beside it.

2 Keep adding to the list until you've thought of as many ways as possible to cut back on the use of fossil fuels.

3 When you've finished, slip your list inside the sheet protector.

4 Tie a string around the dry erase marker and tape the end to the sheet protector.

5 Hang your list where everyone in the family can easily see it every day—such as the refrigerator.

6 Each day, encourage your family to check off on the outside of the sheet protector what they've done to help protect the environment. At the end of the day, erase the marks and start fresh the next day.

THINK ABOUT IT:
How much impact do you think you can have helping the environment during your lifetime?

SUPPLIES

* markers
* poster board or store-bought giant desk calendar

MY YEAR IN WEATHER CALENDAR

You can start this project any time of year—you don't have to wait until January 1 to start! Just jump right in.

1 If you're using poster board, use the markers to draw lines to create a calendar. Be sure to leave nice, big spaces for each of the days.

2 Every week, think about what you've done that week that was impacted by the weather. Maybe you went swimming with friends because it was a really hot summer day. Or maybe you were going to go play tennis but got rained out. Mark your weather experiences each week.

3 If you've created weather measurement tools, mark down any readings you take, such as rainfall or temperature or wind direction.

4 Add in any really big events, too—was there a hurricane on the coast near you? A big blizzard?

5 At the end of the year, look for any trends. You can see seasons by the weather, but what about anything bigger? Was the year rainier than the weather experts predicted? Or was there a drought? By staying in tune with the weather and climate around you, you can learn to anticipate changes in the natural world outside.

TRY THIS! What if you have a friend in another state or country create a weather calendar for their year, too? Then, send each other your calendars (or take photos and send those if your calendars are too big!) at the end of the year. How did their weather experience differ from yours? How was it the same?

absorb: to soak up a liquid or take in energy, heat, light, or sound.

adapt: to make a change to better survive in the environment.

advisory: an official announcement or warning.

air mass: a large pocket of air that is different from the air around it.

air pressure: the force of the gases surrounding the earth pressing downward.

altitude: the height above the level of the sea. Also called elevation.

anemometer: a weather instrument that measures wind speed.

atmosphere: the blanket of air surrounding the earth.

barometer: a weather instrument that measures air pressure.

blizzard: a severe snowstorm with high winds, low temperatures, and heavy snow.

canopy: an umbrella of trees over the forest.

cirrus: a high-altitude cloud characterized by wispy strands.

climate: the average weather in an area during a long period of time.

climate change: changes in the earth's climate patterns, including rising temperatures, which is called global warming. Climate change can happen through natural or manmade processes.

climate zone: a large region with a similar climate.

condense: to change from a gas to a liquid.

contract: to shrink and take up less space.

counterclockwise: in the opposite direction to the way the hands of a clock move.

crop: a plant grown for food and other uses.

cumulus: a low-level, fluffy-looking cloud.

decade: a 10-year period of time.

dense: how tightly the matter in an object is packed.

desert: an area that lacks water, receiving 10 inches or less of precipitation each year.

digital: an electronic way of presenting information as numbers.

Doppler radar: an instrument that uses signals to measure an object, such as a storm, in motion.

drought: a long period of little or no rain.

ecosystem: a community of animals and plants existing and interacting together.

electrical charge: the positive or negative force of matter.

environment: a natural area with animals, plants, rocks, soil, and water.

equator: the imaginary line around the earth halfway between the North and South Poles.

evaporate: to convert from a liquid to a gas.

expand: to spread out and take up more space.

eye: the calm and peaceful center of a hurricane.

fog: a cloud of tiny water droplets near the surface of the earth.

food chain: a community of animals and plants where each different plant or animal is eaten by another plant or animal higher up in the chain.

forecast: to make a prediction of the weather.

fossil fuel: a fuel made from the remains of plants and animals that lived millions of years ago.

freezing rain: rain that freezes on impact with surfaces, such as roads, cars, and the roofs of buildings.

front: the dividing point where two types of air meet.

glacier: a huge mass of ice and snow.

global warming: an increase in the average temperature of the earth's atmosphere.

gravity: a force that pulls objects to the earth.

greenhouse gas: a gas in the atmosphere that traps heat.

hail: pellets of frozen rain.

heat index: the air temperature combined with the humidity in the air.

heat stroke: a condition when your body gets dangerously overheated.

high pressure: an area in the atmosphere where the air pressure and density are above average.

humidity: the amount of moisture in the air.

hurricane: a severe tropical storm with winds greater than 74 miles per hour.

leeward side: the side of a mountain that doesn't get hit by the traveling winds.

low pressure: an area in the atmosphere where the air pressure is less dense than the surrounding air.

mercury: a liquid metal used inside thermometers.

meteorologist: a person who studies the science of weather and climate.

mild: not too hot and not too cold.

molecule: two or more atoms bound together. Atoms are very small pieces of matter that make up everything in the universe.

monsoon: a wind that brings heavy rainfall to southern Asia in summer.

nimbus: a large, gray rain cloud.

Northern Hemisphere: the half of the earth north of the equator.

occluded: describes when a fast-moving front catches up to a slow-moving front.

orbit: the path a planet takes around the sun.

polar: the cold climate zones near the North and South Poles.

precipitation: water droplets that fall to the earth's surface in the form of rain, snow, sleet, or hail.

predict: to say what will happen in the future.

radar: a system that sends out pulses of radio waves that reflect back.

rainforest: a forest in a hot climate that gets a lot of rain every year, so the plants are very green and grow a lot.

rain shadow: an area beside a mountain that gets little or no rain because it all fell on the mountain itself.

recycle: to use something again.

region: a large area of the earth.

renewable energy: a form of energy that doesn't get used up, including the energy of the sun and the wind.

rotation: turning around a fixed point.

scale: a measuring system.

sleet: ice pellets, often mixed with rain and snow, that bounce off the ground.

sound wave: an invisible vibration in the air that you hear as sound.

Southern Hemisphere: the half of the earth south of the equator.

species: a group of plants or animals that are closely related and produce offspring.

sphere: a round object, such as a ball.

stationary: not moving.

stratus: gray clouds that often cover the whole sky.

supercell: a severe thunderstorm with strong movements of air both up and down.

technology: tools, methods, and systems used to solve a problem or do work.

temperate: describes a climate or weather that is not extreme. The temperate zone is the regions north and south of the tropics.

temperature: a measure of warmth or coldness, using a standard value scale.

thermometer: a weather instrument used to measure temperature.

thunderstorm: a storm with thunder and lightning that often produces heavy precipitation.

tornado: a violent, twisting column of air.

tropical: the hot climate zone to the north and south of the equator.

tropical storm: a revolving storm that forms in the tropics.

water cycle: the continuous movement of water from the earth to the clouds and back to the earth again.

water vapor: water in the form of a gas, such as steam or mist.

weather pattern: repeating weather during a number of days or weeks or months.

weather satellite: a small electronic object that circles the earth and sends back pictures of weather patterns.

weather: what it's like outside in terms of temperature, cloudiness, rainfall, and wind.

wind: air in motion.

wind chill: what the combination of air temperature and wind feels like on your skin.

windward side: the side of a mountain that faces into the oncoming winds.

METRIC CONVERSIONS

Use this chart to find the metric equivalents to the English measurements in this book. If you need to know a half measurement, divide by two. If you need to know twice the measurement, multiply by two. How do you find a quarter measurement? How do you find three times the measurement?

English	Metric
1 inch	2.5 centimeters
1 foot	30.5 centimeters
1 yard	0.9 meter
1 mile	1.6 kilometers
1 pound	0.5 kilogram
1 teaspoon	5 milliliters
1 tablespoon	15 milliliters
1 cup	237 milliliters

BOOKS

Fradin, Judy and Dennis. *Tornado! The Story Behind These Twisting, Turning, Spinning, and Spiraling Storms.* National Geographic Children's Books, 2011.

Furgang, Kathy. *National Geographic Kids Everything Weather: Facts, Photos, and Fun that Will Blow You Away.* National Geographic Children's Books, 2012.

Giannella, Valentina. *We Are All Greta: Be inspired by Greta Thunberg to Save the World.* Laurence King Publishing, 2019.

Hamalainen, Karina. *The Extreme Weather and Rising Seas (A True Book: Understanding Climate Change).* Children's Press, 2020.

Sneideman, Josh, and Erin Twamley. *Climate Change: The Science Behind Melting Glaciers and Warming Oceans with Hands-On Science Activities.* Nomad Press, 2020.

Winter, Jeanette. *Our House Is on Fire: Greta Thunberg's Call to Save the Planet.* Beach Lane Books, 2020.

WEBSITES

The National Weather Service for Kids:
weather.gov/cae/justforkids.html

Weather for Kids:
weatherforkids.org

Weather Wiz Kids:
weatherwizkids.com

NOAA for Kids:
oceanservice.noaa.gov/kids

HowStuffWorks:
science.howstuffworks.com/nature/climate-weather

NASA's Climate Kids:
climatekids.nasa.gov/wmenu/weather-and-climate

ESSENTIAL QUESTIONS

Introduction: What is the climate like where you live?

Chapter 1: Why do temperatures change with the seasons?

Chapter 2: How does air pressure affect the weather?

Chapter 3: Why is the water cycle so important to life on Earth?

Chapter 4: What can clouds tell you about the weather?

Chapter 5: What are some ways you can protect yourself from extreme weather?

Chapter 6: Why is climate change a hot topic today?

QR CODE GLOSSARY

Page 3: youtube.com/watch?v=YbAWny7FV3w

Page 13: youtube.com/watch?v=KUU7IyfR34o

Page 37: youtube.com/watch?v=D9PXdpoQpCo

Page 41: nationalgeographic.org/video/droughts

Page 54: climatekids.nasa.gov/cloud-climate

Page 57: weather.gov/jetstream/cloudchart#myModall4

Page 63: weatherwizkids.com/weather-lightning.htm?

Page 65: youtube.com/watch?v=_5TiTfuvotc

Page 76: youtube.com/watch?v=ePL-uOg9hSU

Page 77: climatekids.nasa.gov/climate-change-evidence/?